Nature Theater of Oklahoma's

RAMBO SOLO

53rd State Press
Brooklyn, New York

53SP 4
Published March 2009

53rd State Press
Brooklyn, New York

ISBN 978-0-9817533-3-1

www.53rdstatepress.com

RAMBO SOLO

by Nature Theater of Oklahoma

transcribed and edited by
KELLY COPPER

from a phone conversation between
PAVOL LISKA and
ZACHARY OBERZAN

Rambo Solo received its premiere on August 15, 2008 at the International Summerfestival at Kampnagel – Hamburg, Germany

Featuring:
ZACHARY OBERZAN

Conceived and directed by:
PAVOL LISKA and KELLY COPPER

In conversation with:
ZACHARY OBERZAN

Design by:
PETER NIGRINI

Production managers:
ROBERT SAENZ DE VITERI and GABEL EIBEN

Company manager:
ELISABETH CONNER

US premiere: March 19, 2009 at Soho Rep

Rambo Solo is a production of International Summerfestival / Kampnagel Hamburg in co-production with Kaaitheater Brussels / Workspace Brussels / Buda Kunstcentrum, Noorderzon Festival/ Grand Theatre Groningen, and the Wexner Center for the Arts at The Ohio State University

Hello?
Hi.
Ahhh!
Glad, uh –
That I have a –
A break!
I'm glad that there's –
That I've got really nothing to do and I can just –
FUCK AROUND
And not do anything.
Feel, uh.
I don't know.
I feel.
Restless.
Yeah.
Just feel –
Listless and lethargic and useless and –
Fat.
Yeah.
Uh, but – but for some reason there's uh –
Maybe it's the –
The usual cycles of my –
Chemical? –
I don't know.
But, it just, uh.
I – I – um.
The weather.
I don't know.
But it's just, um.

I uh – just kind of, yeah.
Unin – uninspired and lethargic and –

So I don't know.
That's how I feel.

Uh, so you want me to tell you this – this –
Story of First Blood?
Uh...
Do you, ah –
It's funny!
'Cause I just –
Yeah.
When I came back from Christmas, uh, uh.
In Maine.
I brought back, uh –
My copy of that.
I haven't re-read it again, but I –

I think I read it the first time when I was eleven.
Eleven or twelve.
And I probably read it about eight –
Eight or nine times
Since then.

Uh... oooh!
Sometimes –
Does anyone do that?
Do some people, like –
Finish a book and then
Start right at the beginning?
Yeah, um.

Yeah.
So I've been meaning to read it –
I, er – to read –
Because it's a fast –!
It's a FAST read, too!
I mean normally –
Normally, I'm a slow –
Slow reader.
Uh.
You know, it's –
Takes me –

It – it takes me, uh –
Well 'cause I'm usually reading a few things at –
At once.
But.
(I mean not SIMULTANEOUSLY,
But a few different –)

Ah ha ha!
But, now – but, and
You know –
It takes me like, ah – month to –
Month or two to read –
You know, took me a – took –
Takes me a couple months to read
Tropic of Cancer whatever.
And I'm –

I'm reading Last Temptation of Christ now,
And that's been goin' on for a month, and –
But First Blood I can go through in like –
You know.
Couple days.
Yeah.
Uh.
And it's uh –
It's just –
Uh.
I don't know!
It's a story that I can relate to.
A character that –

Uh.
'Cause I remember, ah –
I think I saw the movie for the first time
Uh – I must have been ten
Ten or eleven.
I think we had free HBO.
Uh.
Every – every once in a while you get –

Maybe – maybe they –
They still do this.
Where you have a –
Normal television cable package.
When I was a kid every once in a while –
To ad – as like an advertisement
To try and get you to sign up for –
For HBO –
Uh.
You get it FREE for a weekend.

And that was a very magical, wonderful time,
'Cause I got to see uh –
(This was—you know, even before VCRs.
So, this was like –
Suddenly movies were being sent into your home...)
And uh.
So.
I remember seeing it like – late at night.
Uh.
I was quite – quite entranced –
By it.
And um –
And then shortly thereafter I saw the uh –
The Novel.
In the – in the supermarket.
Uh – book section.
And um.
The – it had been reissued since the –
Since the movie.
'Cause the book itself came out in '72.
I believe.
And it took ten years
Before the movie was made.
And uh –
But then once the movie was made
A big hit again, they of course reissued the book.
With Sylvester Stallone's picture on the front.

And uh.
So that's when I got it.
And uh – and started my –
Started my
LONG STUDIES
Of – of this book.

Yeahm.
Did you say somethin'?
D'ya – how much detail do you want me to –
Go into?
I can –
You know.
Yeah.
Yeah.
Uh.
Alright.
Let's see.

The book, uh –
Starts out –
I – I – I – I've got –
I remember very specifically.
Both –
For some reason like the —
The opening line of the book
And the closing line of the book.
I – I think I –
I was rambling on about the –
The closing line of the book, which I've
Always been very fond of
Which is the "flooding with love –"
Uh.
"– for the kid" line.

But the – the – the
Opening
Line, too, is always
Uh.

Stuck in – in my head.
'Cause I think the opening line is something like:
Uh – eh:
"He was just some nothing kid."
Like – it's like –
He's describing what Rambo looks like
(The author – you know – solo, third person)
He's describing what Rambo looks like,
And he's just –
Describes him as this –
Kinda this scrawny,
This scrawny –
Kid
Leaning against a – uh.
Gas pump
Drinking a Coke and –
Describes him
As uh – "He was just some nothing kid."

And I always like that line.
And uh.
So anyways.
So the story starts with uh –

With this kid.
This like 22 year old kid.

Not all bulked up on steroids,
You know, it's not –
You know, there's a lot of
HOLLYWOODIZATION
That came in when Stallone got his hands on it.

Uh –
Because, you know most –

What?
Prisoners of war
Probably don't

Come out, you know –
Looking – looking like Stallone.
Unless they –
Unless, you know – uh
In this particular prison camp, you –
You – you know.
They had a lot of
Cybex machines or something.

But.
But um.

So the
So the novel they –
The – this –
(And he's younger, too –
'Cause he's just like –
He's just like 22, and uh.)
He's just uh –
He's in this town.
They're describing this uh –
Yeah.

Course this all gets re –
This all gets –
Should I tell it to you like how –
With – with my –
The way if you were reading the book?
How things slowly get revealed?
Or should I tell it to you with like –
Knowing what I know?

Alright.
Uh.
So, yeah.
I started –
The book starts describing this –
This kid
Saying he's like nothing.

Nothing special.
Just this scrawny-looking bum kinda kid.
22 years old.
Got these shitty clothes, long hair and a beard.
Got like a – the –
Sleeping bag with him
Just like a vagrant.

And um.
In this small town in uh –
Kentucky.
(Yeah, I believe it's in Kentucky.)
Uh.

I think in the film they moved it to
The Northwest,
But in the original… maybe –

(Or maybe it's –
Vice versa.)

But anyway.
Uh.

So – this cop.
Uh.
Named uh – Teasle.
Will – Willfred Teasle.

And meanwhile, too – this is –
So this is like –
Nineteen –
This is like late 60's.
Early – early 70's.
It's like '68.

Uh.
This –
So this small –

Small town sheriff
Ah –
Is out patrolling the streets, and he sees this –
Sees this Bum.
You know, this shady-looking character.
Uh – hanging out.
You know.
And never seen him before.
Doesn't like the looks of him.
Looks like trouble.
You know, doesn't want –
Doesn't want that kind of thing in his town.

So, ah –
He calls him over –
Says "Hey," – you know.
"Who are you? What are you doing?"
And the kid doesn't really answer much.
He just replies –
Somehow without saying anything
Just kinda like –
"Leave me alone."
Just – just real –
Disaffected.
Doesn't want to talk, and –

So.
The cop says
"Well, get –" you know,
"Where – where are you goin'?
Where are you stayin'?"
He says "I don't know. I'm just –"
You know –
'Cause the cop –
He's been through this before, you see –!
Because he's a –
He's been through a lot of towns.
He's been passing from town to town
For the past 6 months

Since he got out of the –
Yeah, the Kid!
Since he got out of the –
The hospital, essentially.
Got out of the army.
Uh.
And uh.
And he's just been hassled by –
Look –
And of course –
And you know this is the –
Politically charged '60s.
And he looks like a Hippie,
And you had all that…
He's been hassled by –
Cops!
COPS!
And he has – and you know –
The authorities
And you know
Cause he looks like a –
A scroungy hippie and –
And uh.
So he – he essentially had this
He's got this history of just going
Just from town to town and
Just sort of bumming around Living –
Sleeping out in the woods and –
And uh.
And cops
Come along and say – you know –
It's like "Hey, Buddy, just keep movin'."
They don't want him in their town.

So anyway.
So this cop, Teasle.
Ah, says:
"Come on. Get in my cruiser and we'll –
I'm gonna take you to the edge of town,

'Cause we don't –
We don't want any trouble
We don't really like your type here, so."
So the Kid, you know –
He thinks for a minute
But he – he gives in.
Just – as usual.
Sorta gets in the cruiser and
And uh –
He drives him to the – to the uh.
Edge of town.

And uh.
And the cop says "Alright, well, you –
Uh. You know – Good luck."
Ah. "Don't come back" kind of thing.
And he turns around, and he starts driving back.
And he looks in his rearview mirror
And what should he see, but – but –
But Rambo!
(That's the kid's name: John Rambo.)
Walking back into town!

And he's all pissed off, like
"Oh what a little –
Little punk!"
'Cause what's goin' on in Rambo's mind
Meanwhile
Is that he's been –
He's been hassled and pushed around by –
By these cops all this time and he's –
Uh.
And he wasn't going to take it anymore!
You know.
And – because – because here's the thing, too:
Rambo is a fucking badass!

RAMBO as we –
As we come to –

Come to learn,
Uh.
Has just been
In a military hospital for about 6 months
Or a year or so
And has just been out for a year
Because he was –
HE was –
A Green Beret!
In the Vietnam War.
And he was –
Captured.
And so he was –
And he was like one of the best of the best.
He was like a young kid but he was just like
Really really good at warfare.
And just really really good
Soldier and a very inventive and just very –
Just a real badass.
Uh.
'Cause the Green Berets –
The Special Forces are just real –
Real badasses.
And he's like –
They're the hardcore.
You know they –
You can just like send them out
In like the middle of a –
Wasteland and they can –
Do – you know they can just
Live off the land and they know how to
Fly every helicopter
And they know how to –
How to uh –
Operate every weapon and they know
How to like make traps and –
Avoid traps and they can –
Run all sorts of –
They're just like these – uh.

The Elite of the Elite.

So, of course, you know the cop
You know –
Looking at this scraggly looking
Hippie kid with a beard and –
You know, un –
And all dirty.
Never – never imagined that there's a –
A war hero.
Essentially.
Because Rambo –
Rambo was captured
And spent uh –
Several months in a
A Vietnam prison camp
Where he was brutally tortured.

Uh.
The tortures included like being tied up.
And um.
Sort of like in a cruc –
Crucifix sort of position
With his, you know – arms –
Up.
And being um.
And the – the evil –
Uh.
The evil –
Vietcong
Torturer would –
Would cut
His body –
Would like cut
Cut his RIBS open.
And uh.
And then he was flogged –
Like whipped from the back and so he –
He uh.

All these –
All these scars all over his back
And all over his chest
From where the –
Where he had been –
WHIPPED AND CUT.
And um.
And they were just – they –
So he was in this prison camp
Where –
For – FOR –
I don't know –
Several months.
And he was – kinda
Being slowly starved to death
Like they wouldn't feed him
For several days and then
He'd be down in a pit and they'd all be –
All the Vietcong would like –
Piss on him and shit on him –
Literally!
And –
And like they wouldn't feed him and then
And then one day
After not like feeding him for like a week,
They threw a snake down and
And so he grabbed the snake and just
Twisted its head off and ate it raw.
And uh.

You know – really –
Really bad conditions.
And uh.
Eh heh. Heh!
So – so Rambo's got all this history of –
So they were –
What happens though is the –
Rambo!
Escaped!

He knew he was gonna DIE in –
In this camp!
Uh.
'Cause they were just –
Essentially just starving him to death.
And torturing him.
And so one – one day
He uh.
While he was out like –
Like carrying dead logs or something,
(He would –
Would – through the –
Through the forest
Which is the job they made him do.)
He somehow took off
Or escaped or something
And uh.
Started the trek back
Down to South –
Down to SOUTH Vietnam.

And apparently it took him like uh –
Uh.
Like a month
Or mo – or –
Two – two months!
'Cause he went –
Like I don't –
He had to go to get back across
Enemy Lines
He has to – he has to
Travel about 300 miles or something.
And uh.
He did this at night.
Because of course there were
Patrols out trying –
Trying to find him.
And it was –
You know he was behind enemy lines.

So.
He'd just travel at night
And during the day he would sleep uh –
He would sleep up in–
Up in trees.

But then after the sh –
Horrible horrible or – like
ORDEAL!
Of – of – of of uh –
Er struggling through the jungle
For –
For – for months!
Half – starved and you know –
Naked and –
And uh.
The army –
Shows up!
At a – at a
You know – US base
In the South and they can't
Believe their eyes
That this guy is like –
Is even alive.
Because he's so – um.
He is just so –
Uh.
Disheveled!

And um.
So then he – and
So he gets the – he – he –
He – he gets the Congressional Medal of Honor.
Uh.
(Which is the highest honor you
The military can – can give you.)
And he just spends a lot of time in like
The hospital
And they –

You know –
Trying to fix him up.
And uh.
Then they let him out!
And so that's where –
That's where the –
You then –
The story
The novel picks – picks up.

All this is kind of revealed
In Rambo's backstory as
As it's being uh.
As the novel goes on.
Yeah.
(Well? –
No, I don't know.
I don't think it—
It's when the cop is seeing him in the?
Like it's not like it's just when the cop
Sees him in the mirror
That all this backstory…)
I think then as – as
As The Kid now gets –

'Cause what happens now in the book is –
So now the cop gets all pissed off
Says all oh you know
"What the fuck!
He's coming back into town!"
So he's – turns around
Comes back and picks him up and –
And says
"Alright, Buddy" you know –
"We're gonna – gonna –
You're resisting arrest" or whatever –
"We're gonna – we're gonna –
Uh arrest you."
Ah.

"I'm gonna take you in."
And uh.
And I remember this –
This is a very good line, too,
In the book
That I remember, um.
'Cause Rambo's –
Rambo's looking at him.
Like – 'cause the cop gets out of the car,
And he's like –
Staring him down.
And he like puts his –
Puts his –
Hand on his – on his gun.
And Rambo's looking at him and
Like in Rambo's mind he's just like –
"You stupid, you silly bastard…" like
"Before you –
Before you even have a chance to like –
Pull your gun,
I could like tear out both of your arms
And like stick your nose up your ass."
And because Rambo's –
You've got to understand –
Is just a fucking badass.
Uh.

And um.
So –
But!
But Rambo again just decides
"Well this isn't the time and place
I'm not gonna – er –
I'm not gonna start a huge
Thing here
I'll just –
Go with him. Uh. I'll –
Fine, I'll just go – go with him."
And um – meanwhile you know all –

All his – his story is being –
Rambo's backstory is being –
Is being revealed.
The – the narrator, you know –
Is revealing his backstory.
And um.

What's the line?
Oh. The line is something like:
Yeah – I can't –
I'm paraphrasing, but it's something like
He's just you know –
"He looked at Teasle and
as Teasle's like –
Hand moved to his gun
And Rambo's thoughts something like
"You silly Bastard, I could –
You know before you even could like
Lift your gun I could
Tear your arms out –"
Some – something.
Something like that.

And um.
Now, and uh – here's –
Here's the thing, too.
Teasle is like a –
Is middle aged.
'Cause it takes –
Teasle's a middle-aged cop.
TEASLE was in –
The Korean War!
And this is something that gets completely –
Completely glanced over
In the movie
But this is a very very important
Aspect of the novel.

He received like the

Distinguished Cross or something
(Which is the SECOND highest medal you can –)
'Cause he was a – he was a
Badass himself!
In the Korean War!

Not as badass as Rambo, of course, but.
He was – he is –
You know, fifteen years earlier
He had been a real badass in Korea.
Um.
And Rambo notices
'Cause what – when –
When they're taking Rambo in to book him
Rambo – Rambo sees in Teasle's office
He sees the – the uh –
He sees his medal there.
So he realizes that uh.
He's a military guy, too.
And um.
So anyway – so they're startin' to uh
Put – put him through the –
The paces and all the cops –
All the cops there are –
Well, some of them are like real,
You know –
Your typical asshole sorta cops with a like
"Oh look at this!
Look what you dragged in.
Look at this bum.
What a – what a scum!"
You know, making fun of the – of his
Disgusting hair and beard and being hippy and
And then some of the other cops
Some of the younger ones are –
Kinda nice are like
"Hey, can't you see this guy is
Kinda crazy? He – "
You know.

Meanwhile, too, of course
None of these people –
You know, no one knows that he's a war hero.
This – as they can tell he's just like this –
He's just kinda this –
Hippy.
You know.

And so
So there's a –
Here's another good line:
They ask him
So – so they're
So they're booking him and
Booking officer's there –
Like ah –
"Why do you – why do you got that beard?"
('Cause he's got – you know
Hasn't shaved for like 6 weeks,
You know. So.)
Uh.
So he says – uh.
"I'm not allowed to shave.
I have a rash on my face
And the doctor says
I can't – I'm not supposed to shave."
And the cop says "Oh! What a –"
You know – "What a – Bullshit!
What the fuck are you talking about?" and then –
And one of the like the younger
Nicer cops says
"No, wait a – wait a minute –
Let's not jump to – you know
Maybe he – maybe it's true,
Maybe it's – maybe that's –
Maybe he does have a rash or something
And the doctor doesn't want him to shave."
Uh.
And then Rambo says:

"No, no. I'm not – I –
I'm lying. I just – I don't –
I don't have a –
That's not the –
I don't have a rash."
And so then the cop says again,
"Okay again, well –
Alright so then –
Alright so okay, I guess –
So why do you got this beard?
Why do you got this long scraggly beard?"
And Rambo says
"Oh I've got – uh.
Doctor told me not to shave because
I have a rash."

And so they're just –
"Well oh alright we get –
You know – what a –
We get –
What a jokester this guy is!"
You know he's just kinda
Fuckin' around with them.
So they start to book him and they
They go and uh.
And this is where things start to get –
They realize things are kinda weird
'Cause they go and they
Have him like –
Take – take a shower and
They see all these scars all over his body
And they're like "Holy shit!
What has this guy
Been into?" you know.

You know his whole body is just –
Is just brutally
Scarred.
And uh.

But he doesn't answer any questions
No, he doesn't tell 'em the
Ah, they find out –
They only find out his name
Because he still has his dog tags.
And so they take his dog tags and realize
His name is John Rambo.
And they realize
That at this point that he had been
A soldier.
But he won't tell them anything about him
Or his history.
So ah.
So he takes a shower.
And they sit him down
And he's naked
Now.
Still.
And.
So he's in like this basement
Of – of the shower
Ah – where the showers are
In the little – basement.
And he's – starts to ah get
These
Flashbacks!
Of you know –
Of being in the prison camp
And – and he couldn't like –
He was just –
The – these cops that are harassing him and
And – and being mean to him
Are saying:
"Alright we're gonna shave you –
Gonna – you know
Gonna cut your hair, cut your beard –"
And
So they've got like a straight-razor

And they're coming over to –
To shave him
And he –
So he starts to have these flashbacks
Of like when the –
When the fucking –
Vietcong guy was coming at him with a little
Sword
That they would cut open his ribs!
And so
And of course he's – you know
He's all heavily – !

He's got post-traumatic stress syndrome.
All that.
He's been through the uh –
War.
Literally.
And um.
So he just –
He – he like starts to freak out
And they GRAB him
They like try and
Hold him down so they can
They can shave him.
And then he just goes –
It gets to be too much
It just –
He just
He freaks out!
He can't take it anymore!
He's having these flashbacks…
He's in this little dank, wet room
People holding him down,
Coming at him with a knife,
And he just –
And he snaps!

And so he just – you know

There's like five cops in the room,
But he is such a badass,
He just like –
And he just like –
Stands up and like –
Grabs –
First grabs the razor outta the guy's hand
And slits him –
Slits him open
Like from his chest down to his groin,
And –
His entrails come out.
And uh.
And then he whips the razor at someone else
And then he just beats the shit outta –
Like the other three cops
And they don't –
They're just bunch of dumb fuckin' –
And Rambo –
Is a fucking badass!

He BEATS them!
HE BEATS THEM!
He just –
Like – in like a matter of seconds
He just –
Just goes through these five cops like nothin'
Because he's just a – you know –
He's like a karate –
Fucking badass!

And uh.
Although he does kill that first cop,
He's just –
Slits him open with the uh –
With the razor.

And so,
Well, so, of course chaos ensues.

So everyone's like "Ah! Holy shit!"
You know
And so he –
Rambo runs out!
And he runs upstairs
And he's – he's naked.
Still.
(Ah, of course in the movie he –
He's not, 'cause they –
Probably found it's too difficult to do, but
This is another –
Interesting detail of the book.)
So he's naked.
And uh,
He runs – he runs out
Of the uh –

What?
Yeah! Yeah, ha!
He's naked!
Heh! And – and uh.
He –
And – this is in October!
Dude – this was in October!
And so it's – uh.
It's – it's – I guess –
Yeah, October in Kentucky so it's pretty –
It's not like REAL cold, but it's –
It's FAIRLY cold, you know,
So you've just gotta think about –
Think about that.

And uh.
So he runs – right into the street!
And being the quick-thinking
Badass that he is,
He sees this guy coming along on a motorcycle.
Grabs the guy on the motorcycle
Throws him off

Jumps on the motorcycle
'Cause the guy kinda slows down
'Cause of –
The naked guy on the street!
He's like "What the fuck?
There's a naked guy on the street!"
And Rambo takes this opportunity
While he's being stared at
You know – to grab the guy and tear him off the –
The bike and –
HE jumps on!
And he takes off
Towards the – towards the edge of town
Towards the mountains.
So meanwhile
Well all the cops are getting themselves together
And Teasle – Teasle hears about –
You know – hears about this.
And they're like
"Oh! Holy shit! Holy shit!"
So.
They all – they're trying to take care of the
Guy that just got his stomach sliced open,
And the rest of them all get in their cruisers and
Go after him.
And so.
They uh.
They chase him to the outskirts –
Of – of town.
In the cruiser.
Then he drives –
Then Rambo drives into the –
Into the woods.
Into the mountains.
And in the –
And then they realize in the cruisers
"Oh we can't follow –
Follow him any further now"
So they get out

They start walking on –
On foot.
Going after him.
And Rambo has to –
He has to ditch the bike
'Cause he's going up the mountain, and the
Bike can't go up there, and so he's
Basically Rambo is –
It's getting near dusk now
And – and Rambo is running –
Like running naked through the –
Er, woods.
And the cops are –
Uh.
And the cops are following him.

And that's kinda the –
End of the first section.

And…
What the cops do now
Led by Teasle –
Teasle's all ripshit about this of course!
He's – he just hates the kid!
He just can't –
He's – like he
Killed one of his FRIENDS now…
And he's this punky KID…
And.
(What?
No he didn't kill –
I think he – he just killed one of them.
I think the other one like he – you know.
Beat the shit outta –
Like broke their arms.
Broke their noses.
But he didn't kill them.)

Uh.

So –
So Teasle and his po – posse there.
Of like six – six or seven deputies are up there
At like the edge of the mountains
And they're – they're wondering –
And the deputies by this point –
And then they get – they get CALLED
Back from the – from the base
And they said
"Hey we found out who this guy is.
This guy is a war hero.
He's a badass war hero."
And um.
And now, too, since it's gone on beyond –
Like the county lines or something
What Teasle SHOULD have done –
Or supposed to do –
Was call in state troopers.
Call in the federal –
The federal Troopers or whatever.

But being a –
Being a man of great pride,
And uh –
And – and pissed off as he is –
Teasle.
He's like "Nothin' doin'.
I'm gonna catch this kid myself."
'Cause now he's like –
Personally –
You know.
Pissed him off.
And killed one of his –
Dudes.

And so.
They camp there.
Overnight.
And they're waiting for the morning.

When they're gonna go in and start hunting him.
And meanwhile then
There's this whole subplot
Because –
The character of Teasle in the book is much more –
Is much more done –
In fact –
It's –
He's probably even fleshed out better than Rambo is
In the book.
Whereas in the movie you –
He's just kind of a – a cardboard figure.
The – the sheriff.
But in the book
Teasle has all this detail drawn
'Cause he's in the middle of a divorce,
His wife's in California, and he's trying to call her
Every
Now and then,
Uh. He's trying to reconcile with his wife,
He's in the middle of this divorce…
He's also trying to reconcile with his –
With his – stepfather
The guy that raised him whose name is Orval.
Who has his dogs
Who he calls up
To have Orval come in
And bring his dogs
'Cause they need the dogs to track Rambo.

So he has to kind of swallow his pride
And ask – ask Orval
Who he has this big fight with about
The way a gun fits in the holster
Uh.
To come out into the woods with his dogs
Says "We gotta go chase this guy."
So Orval says "Okay."
(Orval's 70 years old, but he's in really good shape

And he 's – he works with these –
He's got these –
Bloodhounds. Or some –
Some kind of –
Hound.
But they've – THEY'RE –
They're not actually related, but they're –
Teasle's – Teasle's father like –
DIED.
When Teasle was a kid,
Teasle's father died in a hunting accident.
And Orval raised him.
Orval's kinda like his step-dad.
You see?)
So.
Uh.
So he calls up –
Er – to have Orval come out with his dogs.
And so the next morning
They start out –
They start out to go – go after Rambo just –
With like these six – or seven
Uh – deputies,
And Orval and his dogs and Teasle.
And um.
Meanwhile you know they had other –
They had ov-over –
They had uh –
Other deputies come and bring them supplies,
You know camping supplies and
Ammunition and guns and everything.

MEANWHILE...
What's Rambo doing?
Well, Rambo is running –
You know, run –
Trying to get –
Trying to get away.
And so what he does –

(And uh – plus he's just like running
Naked through the woods
And it's getting cold
And he's naked
Doesn't have any, you know –
Weapons.
Doesn't have any –
Anything.
And so uh –)
He starts
Yelling out all these obscene
Uh
All these like obscene –
Words just like yelling out –
(Although it's – it's funny
'Cause in the book
They don't use any crude –
Crude language…)
But they describe him as like yelling out
Just like disgusting things like:
"Hey! You bunch a cocksuckers!
Hey! You fucking assholes!
Where are you?" – kind of.
'Cause what he's trying to do,
'Cause he had – he thinks that
There must be like –
Hillbilly moonshiners up there.
So he's trying to get the attention of any –
Moon – hillbilly moonshiners.

So, sure enough, he – they
They like –
He's yelling all these kind of obscenities.
And uh –
(But the only way –
You only get the sense then
He's probably –
Figuring out what he does say
Is because then when –

So then when – when he's – when this –
This hillbilly – uh
Father and son
Do
Catch him
Or they – they – they stop him –
They put –
You know they put him in the whole –
They – they turn their flashlights on him and
And uh –
And like the father says "What's –
What the fuck are you doin'
Runnin' around here sayin'
Uh – people – cocksucker?"
or somethin'.
I don't know.
Heh ha ha!
Ah and Rambo says
"Ah, I was just –"
You know,
"I was just tryin' to get your attention.
Just tryin' to get some attention.
Some –"
(This part of the book has always –
Seems a little weird to me
'Cause I would always wondered
How Rambo would –
Would have known!
That just by running around
Through the woods
Screaming
Obscenities
That you would –
That that would like –
Bring out
The hillbillies!
But apparently it does.
And it – and it worked for him.)
And um.

So.
Uh.

So.
Uh.
So yeah.
So he – so he gets like caught in the –
His –
So this hillbilly
And his hillbilly son are like
Shining these flashlights on him and
They live in –
They live in the woods. Yeah.
'Cause like Rambo figures
"Oh they must have a still up here!"
It's like – making moonshine
So he says
"Hey!" you know.
"You gotta help me out, I'm uh.
I'm on the run from the – from the law,
As you can see, I – you know
I don't have any clothes or anything
I need you to give me –
I need you to give me some clothes
And a rifle."
And they're like "Aw!
Like hell! Bullshit!
Like I'm gonna give you –
You know, I'm gonna kill you!"
And he says "Well, you know
The cops are gonna be following me through here
At – you know, in the – in the –
In the morning
They're gonna be coming through with dogs.
And they're gonna find your still,
So either you help me out, and I'll –
I'll go like around
I'll go around, so –
You know, over here –

The other way so the can't –
Won't find your still,
Otherwise they're gonna –
They're gonna find your still."
And the old man spits or somethin'
And he's like
"Ah! Goddamnit.
I guess he's got me there!"
So he sends the kid back to uh –
To get him some clothes and a –
And a rifle.

And uh.
And then the old man
He's got like a
Big jug of – of
Of his own stuff, and he –
And so while they're sittin' there
Rambo and the old man have – start –
Start drinkin' the – the stuff.
And then the kid comes back
And he starts drinkin' the stuff, too.
So they're all drinkin' the stuff.
And uh – the –
The guy gets really friendly probably
'Cause he's getting drunk, and –
And so he says um –
He gives Rambo his own –
His OWN rifle
(Which is a really good rifle
And it's got a bit of luminous paint
Dabbed at the end of the, uh –
At the end of the site, so that he can –
You – so that you can –
You can aim well at night.)
And he gives him a – a red
Handkerchief tied – tied to –
With uh – with cartridges.
With bullets.

And.
Um.
He gives him like jeans
And –
A shirt
And then an over – like a red
Uh –
Wool overshirt.
(Well, you know what –?
I think –
I think in the –
I think he might actually give him –
Yeah!
He give –
Might actually give him his coat himself.
Or – or his –
The kid brought it.
I can't remember but –)
But – but Rambo was kinda pissed
Too
'Cause the kid didn't bring any socks
And he thinks he –
The kid did it on purpose.
Just 'cause the kid didn't like him.
Uh.
And the boots are too big.
But he solves that by –
By putting –
Shoving leaves in the –
In the toes.

Oh!
Oh and he also asks
Them for –
He says
"Bring a can of kerosene."
And he says
"I'll douse – I'll douse the clothes
And the – like with – kerosene."

Before he puts on –
Because that that –
Something about that will
Throw the dogs off, too.
Like it won't help –
It won't help him or something
But it will help throw
The dogs off from coming near
Their still or something.
I don't know.
So.
So.
So.
So he gets clothes and a gun.
He gets himself clothes and a gun.
Rambo does.
You following?
And – ah.
So he takes off again.
Deeper into the woods.
Some – so – so now it's like the next day.
And – and the dogs are –
Teasle and his gang of –
Of deputies and Orval are
Are starting to close in on him.
And um.
They get a helicopter out there too!
And –
You know
Rambo can hear the helicopter coming there
And he can hear the dogs barking and
And he's runnin' and runnin'
Trying to get away
And he knows that they're closing in on him.
And at – and at one point he –
He uh –

He has to run across this big open field.
And there's um –

And so he's running across this open field
As fast as he can.
Hoping that the helicopter doesn't come
While he's running across
But then – it does!
It does!
It comes!
So he – he like just like the last second
He jumps under this – like fallen pine tree.
To hide himself, so they can't see him.
And he's really scared
Because he's got this red thing –
Like this red, woolen shirt on and he's –
He's just sure they're gonna see him and
You know –
Shoot him from the – from the
Air or something, but um –
That's –

Somehow they miss him.
Uh.
They don't see him.

And um.
So he starts running again, and um.
He uh.
Let's see.
He comes to –
Oh yeah!
So this is the really good –
This is the really good part.
Because –
Ah –
He –
Um –
(Wait, does he say that? –
No, no he doesn't.)
He –

Yeah!
This is a really good part
'Cause what happens is –
So he knows they're closing in
The dogs are coming.
And uh.
And the helicopter's coming
And he –

But he –
Rambo kinda screws up, because he kinda
Er – leads himself to a –
To a dead end.
He thinks he's goin' eh
The right way
Taking his bearings from this and that
(The way that Green Berets do, whatever.)

But he comes to the –
Like sheer –
This like hundred foot sheer
Cliff.
And there's no way –
There's no way
Back.
There's like oh – if you go –
There's only one way back
And then he'd run right into them.

And meanwhile
And the helicopter's comin'!
But he's like totally –
Totally stuck.
And so what he does –
Is he takes the uh.
He says "Ah," just uh – you know
"I've gotta try to climb down this sheer –
Cliff!"
And so, he sticks the gun

His rifle in the – into the belt.
And uh
Starts to slowly
Carefully
Climb down this very
Sheer
Cliff.

And as he's going down
He's maybe like a quarter of the way down
And – and of course the helicopter shows up.
And the helicopter starts uh –
Shooting at him!
And –
Every time it shoots
It gets – eeh.
Like a little closer.
You know the bullets are getting a little
Little close
While he's trying to climb down.
I mean he can hardly move
This like this really
Sheer
Face
Of a cliff
And so
Here he is –
You know on the –
Hanging
By his fingernails
By the side of this cliff
Helicopter's there shooting him

Course the –
They're not s'posed to shoot him!
You know, they're s'posed to just like
Bring him in
But of course you know all the
Cops are pissed because

He killed one of –
He killed one of them, and so
They're just out to kill
Rambo, you know.

And so – the – the
The shots keep gettin' closer
And real – Rambo realizes
"Okay, once the –
Once the –
The helicopter pilot
Realizes how to –
How to steady the helicopter here
The guy's gonna be able to get a clear shot
And I'm gonna be
Gone!"
But – but he – ah –
Is just on the side of a fucking cliff!
And so he looks down,
And he sees there are pine trees.
There are pine trees
Maybe like ah –
Uh –
You know – 20 feet below him or so
Big pine trees.
And so –
He –
Knowing that like he's –
Well, he's gonna get –
He's gonna die in the next
5 seconds if he doesn't do something
He just JUMPS!
He jumps
Off of the cliff.
Just pushes himself off the cliff.
And tries to jump
And
So that he FALLS
Onto top of the pine trees

You know these pine trees are like 75 feet high.

And so he lands on top of the pine trees
And just like falls
So they kinda break his –
He falls THROUGH the pine trees,
So it kinda breaks his fall
But not –
Not very –
Not very well.
You know, it's not a very pleasant
Experience.

And as he's falling,
He breaks his ribs.
That's his first major –
Injury.
And as I read the book, I keep very
Close tabs uh – uh –
To myself in my own mind of
The various injuries that he's sustaining.
And ah –
(And again the mov—
The movie does a shitty job
The movie just –
Cuts his arm or something
So they can –
So that he can –
Sew it up
With his knife, but that's uh –
That's not in the book.
In the book he breaks his ribs.)

And so he falls through the trees,
And he finally
And he's falling through the branches
And he breaks his ribs
And uh he finally hits the –
You know – hits the bottom.

He hits the ground, and –
(No! He finally stops himself!
He – he stops himself!)
'Cause – and –
And he climbs down
The rest of the way.
Uh –
To like – where the lowest branches are.
But they're still like twenty – twenty –
Twenty feet off the ground
But because of his badass paratrooper training
He knows how to –
Even with his broken ribs
He can jump –
He jumps from the –
Like twenty feet down and like –
LANDS
And does a perfect somersault.
And – and he's fine.

And then
He uh –
He takes –
And he shoots back!
At the uh –
Helicopter dude
And shoots HIM.
And so he kills the dude in the helicopter.
What?
Yeah, he falls –
He falls – he falls out.
Uh.

In the movie, too there's another –
Stupid thing,
'Cause –
In the – in the MOVIE
What happens is Rambo –
'Cause Rambo doesn't have a –

A gun.
And he's –
Rambo in the movie is made much more –
Sympathetic.
He's made much – much more into a
Complete hero.
There's – you know, like –
Nev— never does anything wrong.
Never kills anyone, and
Intentionally, or –
And so – yeah, in the –
In the movie he – he –
He grabs a fucking rock!
And throws the rock at the helicopter!
And that –
Rattles the helicopter
And the guy falls out, but –
But – but, no.
In the – in the book he shoots the guy.
Uh – he shoots the guy
Who is trying to shoot him.
In the helicopter
And he falls out.
And then the helicopter takes – takes off.
Like "Holy shit!
We – we're getting shot at!"

And then Rambo runs over
And uh –
To the guy who –
Who fell outta the helicopter.
Go and grab his supplies.
He grabs his jacket and his
Service Pistol and um
He finds –
The guy has Smoked Meats
He has like this little pouch on his belt
Full of smoked meats,
And he – he's –

Of course Rambo's just famished!
And so he eats those like all –
It's just –
Stuffing the smoked meat in his mouth.
And his canteen!
– his canteen.

Yeah!
Like beef jerkey!

And uh – AND takes –
He takes the guy's – uh
Pants belt!
Not only like his – like his –
His gun belt he takes
But he also takes the guy's like –
Trouser...
Belt.
Because what he does is, in order to fix –
'Cause he knows he's broken his ribs,
And so he takes this –
Belt, and he –
Cinches it!
– up above his ribs.
And that helps kinda hold them –
Hold them in and – and um –
Relieves – re – reduces some of the – the –
The pressure.

'Cause his –
'Cause his rib is like pinching into his –
Into his lung.

So –!
He starts – and so he's –
So then he runs
He runs out to set up this ambush.
'Cause he knows the dogs and Teasle
And his whole gang are about to come, and um –

Are about to come, and uh –
To that –
To the top of the cliff where
He just was!
And so what he does is
Being the smart – you know –
The strategic uh –
Green Beret guy that he is, he knows
All the arts of warfare,
He positions himself very well
Very – very well
At the – at the edge of the forest,
At the bottom of the – of the cliff.
And what happens is –
So that all of the –
So the dogs and the –
And the six or seven deputies
And Teasle and Orval show up
At the top of the cliff,
And they're like looking around,
And they're like "What the – ?
Like where did he?
Where did he go?
What – what happened?"
And then they see the body down,
Of like the other –
The helicopter guy…

Meanwhile though!
Rambo's positioned himself out –
And he starts pickin' them off!
One by one
With his uh –
With his – with his rifle.
And the deputies – they just like
"Holy shit!" they're like –
"Hit the deck!"
And they all start returning the fire,
And they're just like –

'Cause these are all like untrained –
These are just like local hick dep –
Deputies.
They're not trained in any kind of warfare
Or anything.
But they just – they're –
They just like scream! They like –
They – they literally –
One of them literally shits his pants.

So like all the guys that –
They're just like –
Firing!
And Teasle's –
(Who's got some war experience)
Is yelling like "Stop! Stop!"
You know –
"You're just wasting your ammunition!"
You – you can tell everyone's just
Freaking out and firing…

(But not in the movie.
He doesn't shit his pants in the movie.
No, no.
But – but in the book…)

So they all just like hit the deck
And they start uh –
And they're just shooting, shooting shooting!
And like some of them are even like
Pumping out their –
Like before – before even pulling the trigger,
They're just like pumping the rounds out.
And it's like something that happens –
Like when you're in a –
Inexperienced.
In – in – in a gunfight.
You just like – keep like –
Pumping the – the rounds,

But you're not actually pulling the trigger.

Anyway.

And so after like five minutes of just
This barrage –!
And meanwhile –
So Rambo shot a couple –
Rambo shoots like a couple –
He shoots –
Well, he shoots the dogs.
The dogs fall over the cliff.
Orval has a fit;
Orval gets up and tries to go and save –
Save one of the dogs from falling over the cliff,
So Rambo shoots him;
Shoots a couple of the other deputies…
And everything's just complete chaos.
Kills 'em?
Yeah.
Well – well, no…
Orval's not quite dead.
Orval's been shot in the chest,
But he's not dead yet.
But he kills a couple of the deputies,
And he's killed the dogs.
And uh –

Oh! here's another good line I – I –
I remember, something like be –
Before all the shooting –
Starts or something, like –
Where they're trying to figure out where he went,
Or where he – where he could have gone, and –
And at some point like
Teasle says something like:
"Oh – in the amount of time you guys spent like
Fucking around now, wasting time,
Like he could have taken a –

He could have dug a hole,
And taken a shit,
And buried it, and been gone by now."

I've always liked –
I've always liked that –
That line.
It always really cracked me up.
Especially as like – an eleven year old, especially.
Just kinda the absurdity of that line.
That Rambo could have like –
Dug a hole –!
('Cause you try to picture it! Yeah!)
Like taken a shit!
Covered it up!
And – and like GONE!
While they were fucking around…
Like the – the luxury of that!
That he would have had the luxury of that time.
While the dumb deputies were
Just like fucking around,
While on the run from them,
He would have had the time to –
Like dig a hole and take a shit.

Huh! I always liked that.
I've always been – I'd like to use that.
In my own life.
That – that metaphor.
At some point.
(If I can…)
So.

Any time someone is late or is like
Twiddling around or something, and I'd –
"Goddamn it, Bobby! I could have –
Dug a hole,
Taken a shit,
And covered it

By the time it took you to do that!"
Yeah.

Yeah.
Anyway, so –
And it's startin' to rain!
It's startin' to rain, too, and it's –
And this rain is turning into a torrent,
And so…

Because they're up on like the top of this –
This cliff!
It's becoming – it's like the –
And there's like this –
Flash – flash flood!
And like not – not only are they getting like –
You know Rambo's pickin' them off
One by one,
But the water is rising, it's like –
'Cause they're in like this trough.
And so.
There's like this fast flash flood.
Half of them are wounded.
Orval's been badly wounded in the chest.
The water is rising, uh –
So Teasle realizes:
"Okay – we gotta retreat.
We gotta back up."
And so they –
They start to try to work their way back
Down the cliff,
While staying low so Rambo can't shoot them.
And they're tryin' to –
They're tryin' to bring Orval down 'cause
Orval's 70 years old,
And he's been shot in the chest.
And they're trying to take care of him
And bring him down.
And it's just chaos,

'Cause it's getting dark, and so –
And it's just pouring rain, and uh –
Orval has to –
He takes his shirt off to – to cover up –
Uh – cover –!
TEASLE takes off his shirt to cover up
Orval's wound.
So he's really cold, and it's raining.
And uh –
He's trying to get –
Bring Orval down, and uh –
Meanwhile like Rambo's pickin' off
Couple more of them,
Shooting them,
While they're trying to get down,
And – and one of them,
McGolf I think his name was…?
Or I forget which –
Like kinda – well –
Mitch!
Yeah, Mitch!

Mitch takes off, like ahead of them, and
And – and Teasle's all –
Teasle's all pissed, 'cause like –
"Well, goddamn it! Why isn't Mitch –?!
How come no one's here helping me bring –
I'm trying to carry Orval down –
No one's, no one's helping me!"
And he's really really pissed, and it's raining,
And everything's just chaos –
And they're getting shot at,
And then – he's trying to bring Orval down,
And then, uh –
Mitch –
Mitch comes back!
And Orval – uh –
Teasle is so pissed off! He's a –
(Here's another detail from Teasle's past:

He's a boxer. He's a trained boxer...)
So soon as – soon as Mitch, uh –
Gets there,
He grabs him,
And punches him!
Really hard in the face!
And knocks out his teeth!
Mitch's teeth!
Yeah!

And Mitch is like:
"What the fuck!? What are you doin' hittin'!?"
"What the – Why'd everyone run off
And leave me here with Orval?"
And he said
"No...! No, Will, I didn't leave you.
Everyone else ran off;
I came back here to help you!"
And so then –
And so then Teasle feels bad,
'Course then the two of them together try and –
He's –
Now that Mitch's –
Teeth are all fallin' out and
All bloody,
And they're tryin' to bring Orval down
And then the –
The uh –

Meanwhile now!
Rambo, though –
Rambo knows he's got them on the run!
And so Rambo heads back up after –

Well, no!
Here's the thing!
'Cause Rambo –
Rambo at this point knows
(And this is where Rambo kinda screws up!)

Because he –
What he should have done –
If he had just taken off at this point,
Just let it go –
And just let Teasle go –
He coulda probably gotten away.
But he was so pissed at Teasle
For startin' this whole thing,
He wanted to go after and kill Teasle.

So he starts chasing Teasle now!
He knows he's got him on the run.
And so –
Uh –
He goes back after –
He goes back after Teasle and then –
So Teasle and Mitch are trying to get Orval
Down,
And –
It's raining, and they let – they –
Teasle loses hold of him,
And Orval gets swept over the side
So he's dead, too –
And uh –
So Teasle, Orval, and Mitch are retreating.
Yeah –
Orval – yeah.
Mitch and –
All the other deputies kinda ran – ran –
Ran off ahead,
Scared,
And –
(That were still alive)
And Orv –
And Teasle and Mitch are trying to bring
Orval's body
Down off the cliff
Back the way they came
But the torrents –

The flooding is too much, and they –
And they – he goes over –
They lose Orval.
Orval goes over the side.
So now – now to Teasle it's –
He's –
It's like – his dad is dead.
He's getting –
Like his DAD is dead!
It's getting very personal.

Yeah! Yeah!
'Cause he's –
You know, they're outta ammo,
He's there –
It's – it's – just chaos.
His whole posse's been – been –
Been killed.
And um.

So.

He and – he and Mitch
Then are just –
Are the only ones left.
And he –
And he –
Uh –
He KNOWS
That Rambo's coming after them.
They can hear him, or they –
Somehow they know:
Rambo's coming after them.

And so they're like sitting under a tree,
And it's still pouring, and – and – and –
And um.

So.

Teasle says “Okay –
Alright. I’m gonna go out
And check. Just like – look.
Look around.
See – see which way we should go
And see what –
What’s going on.”
And so he goes off for a little bit.

When he comes BACK…
Mitch is gone.
(It’s still raining. Yeah.
It’s still raining…)

He comes back.
Mitch is gone.
And he’s lookin’ around, and
Suddenly he hears a –
From like –
From the bushes –
He hears – he hears uh –
“Will! He’s got me!
Ugh!” And –

While – while Teasle was out
Kinda scouting around by himself.
Rambo was tracking them,
Found Mitch –
And thought he had killed him,
Thought he had stabbed him?
To death?
But –
And was waiting – and was waiting
With Mitch’s body
For Will to come back
And then he was going to kill – Will.
(This was Will – Will Teasle.)

BUT!

But Mitch –
Mitch wasn't – wasn't dead!
And so he warns him.
He says uh "Will! He's got me!"
And then Rambo's like
"Woahell fuck! I thought you were dead!"
And then he like snaps his neck again,
Or something.
BUT –
That's – that's it for – Tea –
Teasle's at his breaking point now,
And
He screams!
'Cause he's just – uh.
He – he –
He's out half naked now
Out in the woods
Without – you know.
His whole posse's been murdered,
He knows he's being hunted now by Rambo,

He just goes berserk.

He just starts to scream and run.

Yeah.
And so – and Rambo's really close to him,
And Rambo –
So Rambo starts chasin' after him.
And Teasle knows that Rambo's
Right behind him,
And he's just goin' bzz –
He's just screamin' – you know all –
ALL sort of military training has gone –
Out the window now, for Teasle.
He's just like –
Screaming like a baby,
Running through the woods, just –
'Cause he just can't –

He's just – s-s-s
He just snapped, you know?
And uh –
Rambo's really close to him.
Of course, Rambo's –
Having some trouble because
His ribs are broken,
So he can't –
You know –
But he's still –
Runnin' pretty fast and doin' –
He's do –
Doin' everything that a good
Green Beret should do, but –
But he is –
He's a bit slowed down by his broken ribs.

And he keeps getting close –
Close to –
Close to Teasle,
But he just –
Keeps losin',
Teasle keeps get – gettin' away from him.
And Rambo –
And it occurs to Rambo, too,
(And it's still raining)
And uh –
Rambo's thinking to himself:
"You know, this is really –
I'm wasting a lot of time.
This – strategically – is very stupid for me
To chase after this one guy just to kill him
Out of revenge.
When I should be using this time to get away."
But he – but he's just still
Driven to like uh –
"I gotta go get him! I gotta go get him!"
And he –
So he almost gets him a few times

And – and uh,
But Teasle keeps – keeps getting away from him.
And then finally,
He ends up –
Teasle –
Like looks up and realizes
He's at the – ah –
He – he's –
He sees barbed wire.
He realizes he's back at the road.
He's back at the edge of town.

And he – he made it.
You know?
He got – he got outta the woods.
He escaped Rambo.
And –
And uh – and Rambo –
Meanwhile then – uh –
And right –
Right near the EDGE
Of the field, too, there
Between there are bram –
Are like these –
R – ram – rambles?
Brambles?
(Like in Central Park – what do you –
What are the –?
Bram – Brambles?)
THORNS!
Like all these THORNS!
And uh –
So like to finally get through
At the end, just –
Teasle had to pull himself
Through these thorns,
And Rambo's pulling himself through the thorns, too,
But Teasle gets out, and he –
Gets out and he gets to the road.

In time.

It's –
I think it's day, by this point.
This has been going on all night,
And Ram – Rambo –
(And this is one of the –
Most poignant –
Poignant parts of the book, too…)
Like – so Rambo after all this –
Just ex – expending all this energy that he should have
You know – been used to –
To get away, and it –
Ribs are broken, and –
And he's –
He's hungry and wet and exhausted,
And everything, and he should have been –
You know – just tried to get away,
But he's –
Wasted all this time to go after Teasle,
And then in the end he doesn't even get him,
And it says like –
"Rambo put his –
Put his head in his hands and wept."

Uh.

And I think –
That's the end of Part One in the book.

Uh –
I have to go to the bathroom.
Uh –
But I'll be right back, so hold on.

INTERMISSION

Okay, I'm back.
You ready for more?

Uh –
So now the second part of the book begins.
And
Uh –
So now, of course, by this point,
You know – the state police have been called in.
It's, I guess, a big national news story
This –
Guy's on the run
In the woods,
He's killed these cops, and –
He's a war hero, blah blah blah…
This story.
And uh –
So they set up this –
The federal
Troopers, and – and uh –
The army's been called
The national guard
Has been called –
Called in, and uh –

Teasle's in pretty bad shape now,
You know, 'cause he's –
Uh –
He's just been through this hell
And um,
The doctors are telling him to like –
"Take it easy,"
"You're gonna get –" you know:
"Go and like –
Lie down, you gotta take these pills."
An' I guess his like heart is –
Palpitating and stuff,
But he's too –
He's too driven by this whole thing now,

And now his like –
Life calling to go and get –
To get –
The Kid, as he – as he calls him in –
In his head.
Whenever Teasle thinks of him
He thinks of him
As The Kid.

Yeah,
He's in the hos –
Well, he's in like this field hospital
That's set up at this base camp
That they've set up
Outside of the – at the woods.
Where they're gonna go and try and
Track him again.

But then, now,
Of course they brought in all this –
Heavy
Machinery
And hardware and army people,
And helicopters to go and –

AND –
And they bring in Sir Colonel – uh –
Samuel Trautman.
(Who was Rambo's commanding officer
In Vietnam,
And the one guy that –
In – in the world! –
That Rambo –
Uh –
Trusts.
'Cause he was like a father figure to –)

Because by now they –
You know they've done a –

They've done a –
They've done a check on Rambo,
They – everyone KNOWS now,
Who he is and where he's
From.
What his story is.
And so.
You know, and –
It's been brought to the government's attention.
They're sending in, you know –
State troopers and everything, and so
The army sends –
SENDS
Colonel Trautman.

Uh –
He wasn't as good as – he tried –
He trained him.
Colonel Trautman trained him
At Fort Bragg.
Uh –
Well his – well, in the BOOK –
In the BOOK it's just been –
It's just been like –
Uh –
A year or so since
Since – since –
Since Rambo escaped from the prison camp.
In fact in the book, I think
It's still –
Like the war is probably still going on.

Um.

So, anyway.
Colonel Trautman shows up there.
And uh –
He's – says:
"Yeah, well the army's sent me here –

I'm here you've got – you know –
One of my – one of my boys here,
Causing some trouble, and uh –
Let's see what we can do
To try and get him back."
So –
Immediately this sort of
Rivalry starts up
Between Trautman and Teasle
Because
Trautman is very
PROUD of Rambo –
He likes him!
And he's almost –
I mean, of course he doesn't want the –
He's not –
Glorifying the fact that he killed a bunch of cops,
But he is –
He does kinda have this attitude like:
"Huh. I'm surprised he let YOU live!
Like –
Rambo's the Best of the Best.
He is just –
You know –
You – you –
You should never fuck around with Rambo.
What's the matter with you?"

And so –
So there's kinda this rivalry
Between Teasle and Trautman.

And Teasle's like:
"What the hell are you doin' here?
Do – do you want him to win?
You act like –
Like you want him to –"

And Trautman's like:
"Well, no, no – I don't wanna –
You know –
I know he's broken the law.
We gotta bring him in, but –
But I don't want – you know.
You – you –
We shouldn't kill him.
We just gotta capture him, and –
And bring him in.
Because he – he's a good guy"

And of course Teasle
Just wants to kill him.

So –
Uh.
Rambo
Meanwhile has now, after –
You know, wasting all that time
And energy trying to catch Teasle has –
Gone, you know –
Has gone back,
Further into the woods.
And he's really feelin' like shit.
And uh –
He's really hungry.
And uh –
He's hidin' out in this cave,
And he's really hungry
And he sees
An owl fly by a few times,
And realizes that the owl always
Perches on the same branch.
And so he shoots – uh –
He shoots the owl.
And um – he –
He, uh –
(I always liked this part, too,

'Cause it describes how –
That he like
Prepares the meat,
And he cuts off the –
He pulls the feathers out
And cuts off the
Head
And the wings
And the feet
And – and guts it,
And puts it on a – little spit, and
Cooks it.
And – but he says it tastes really bad.
It tastes worse than he thought it would,
And he wishes he had salt and pepper.)

Um.
And uh –
And his lungs are really bothering him now,
From being – you know 'cause –
The – the – the uh –
Broken ribs.
And he's getting – got –gotten – getting like –
Pneumonia,
He's got all this phlegm and stuff.
And he's coughing up all this phlegm.
He's – you know – in pretty bad –
Pretty bad shape, but he's –
But he keeps telling himself:
"Oh, you're not that –"
You know –
"In the war you could have gone longer,
You could have gone –"
You know, he –
He's always kinda –
He's all tough on himself!
He's always kinda like –
"Ah! –
Don't be a –

Don't be such a sissy!
In the war you coulda handled this."

And uh –
And he knows – he – he –
They – they know – they know, too –
That he's picked up –
That he took the Walkie-talkie from
The guy he killed in the helicopter.
So Trautman knows that, um –
That he's listening in
To –
To the radio signal that everyone's –
To the –
To the Walkie-talkie business.
He knows that Rambo's listening in.
So he tries to contact Rambo.
And –
You know,
So Rambo's listening in to all the –
The Walkie-talkie stuff going on,
The police positions and everything, but –
And –
But then he hears Trautman's voice come on!
And they think – "Ah, well –
He's not gonna break –
He's not gonna break
Radio Silence
Just to talk to Trautman,
'Cause then we'll be able to get a fix on him,
On his location."

But he does!
Rambo takes –
Takes a chance!
And he talks to Trautman for a minute,
And says like –
"I didn't – this isn't my fault.
They – they started it. The –

The cops' fault."
Uh –
Eh –
And Trautman –
And like –
And they talk a little about –
Bit about the old days
And Rambo's nostalgic,
And says "Ah, they're all dead, sir.
The –
Rest of the troops is all –
Of the troops are all dead.
I'm the last one."
And Trautman says:
"Come on, just turn yourself in."
And Rambo –
Yeah, Trautman turn –
Tells Rambo to turn himself in.
But Rambo's defiant!
He says "No,
I'm not going to turn myself in,
He –"
(Referring to Teasle) says –
"He – he drew first blood.
He started it. It's his –
He started the war –
He shouldn't have –
He shouldn't have
Pushed me.
He asked for a war and now he's
Getting one."
Kinda thing.

And um.

Uh –

So this is – so – so he –
He – Rambo knows that like

All these hun –
Like hundreds of
Searchers and uh – ah –
So now all the townspeople,
Ah –
From like –
All over.
It's just –
You got all these hicks
From like all over –
The neighboring counties.
Anyone with like a rifle
Has been called in.
Or is – or has been –
Is coming up
To look for Rambo.

And they know it's –
It – like Teasle knows –
It's just become a –
Like uh –
This huge circus!
You've got all these hicks –
Hicks now out in the woods
With rifles
Trying to find Rambo.

He – he SHOULD
Be in the hospital.
The doctors say
"You should –
You gotta get some rest.
You gotta stay in the hospital."
('Cause his heart's palpitating and –
All this shit.)
But he's not –
Uh –
He's – has NONE of it.
He's gonna be –

He wants to be right there on the front lines
He wants to go back in himself and –
Get Rambo!
But he's NOT
Very healthy himself now.

Anyway –
Uh.
So what –
What Rambo does is –
(He's very very clever.)
His plan to get past –
He knows that like he can't keep goin'
Forward or something,
And that he's being encircled by
(Or wait – no.
First he goes through the rats…?)
What?
Yeah – oh! –
Okay!
He um.
Rambo's –
First, he –
Yeah.
He's trying to uh –
Oh yeah!
This is how he does it:
Rambo's really clever.
He knows that he's being encircled by –
By not only the –
Uh –
'Cause they've got national guards,
They've got the army,
They've got the police,
They've got these patrols of –
Hick – you know –
R-r-rednecks out –
All everyone –
Like –

Yeah, Volunteers.
All out lookin' for him, and so.
He knows he's being encircled, so
What he does is he uses one of his
Really badass –
Eh – uh –
Tricks!
Green Beret tricks.

He – he finds this stream,
And –
He covers –
He goes –
He gets –
In the stream.
It's got like a soft
Stream bed with dirt –
Bed, and he covers himself
Completely
With the mud.
Underwater!
He goes underwater,
He like – essentially –
He buries himself.
Under the stream,
And he takes like a – uh – er –
Uh – a reed or something
That he can breathe through.
And –
So that –
So that –
The search line
Will come and go right over him.

And at first he –
And so he tries to time it
So he doesn't have to stay down there too long.
He's trying to time where he knows
When they – they'll be coming along.

And so he –
He buries himself under there,
And I mean you know he's –
Breathin' through the tube and it's –
His ribs are –
You know his ribs are really killing him!
And uh – eh –
And he can't hear anything, too!
He can –
(Well, he can hardly hear anything.
Of course he's – he's underwater.
So he can hardly hear when people –
You know –
If people are going by or not.)
And he's startin' –
He starts to panic, and –
And he – and he starts to –
You know –
It's like an HOUR's gone by.
And he – he starts to think:
"Maybe they already went by.
Maybe they –
Maybe they already went by
Maybe this –
Maybe they're all – you know –"
Anyway, he starts to panic,
And he's just about to –
Like –
Uncover himself.
('Cause he's pretty uncomfortable, too!
You know, he's been under –
He's like – you know, like –)
When all of a sudden
He hears people coming.
He hears the searchers coming.
And they start to come,
And start to cross the stream,
And of all things, one of the –
One of the guy – one of the searchers stops

And like stands on top of his chest.
In the stream.
And Rambo's like
"Holy! –"
And his – you know –
His – standing on his –
On his broken ribs.
And Rambo's like, you know –
Screaming, you know –
Silently.
In pain.
While this guy's standing on his broken ribs,
And he's buried under the mud.
Under the stream, but eventually –
The guy – the search party goes on.
So in other words, the search –
The search line moves –
Moves right over him.
And so when he's sure that they're –
That they've gone past –
He uh –
He un–
He uh – digs himself out of the mud,
And starts heading down,
You know – starts heading back
A – away from the –
Search line as they keep moving in.

Now what happens is uh –
We –
(And here we see a –
Here we see a – a very – very
Human
Side of Rambo) because
He uh – he –
Going down– he's kind of almost free.
He's almost kind of to the edge –
Edge of the woods where he can get out,
And this KID – !

This like young,
Like 13 year old kid
Who's out there with his dad or somethin'
Searching for – you know –
Is part of the volunteers.
Uh – he –
He stumbles upon this kid!
And the kid's like terrified –
Because like –
And – and – but rather than –
What Rambo could have done
Is just like kill the kid and kept –
Kept going!
But he doesn't –
He doesn't kill him.
He thinks – he's like –
Some – some part of –
Some noble part
Of Rambo says like
"Sh – shouldn't kill kids!"
So he just, uh –
He just keeps going,
But of course, then the kid starts
Screaming his head off says
"Ah! I see him! I see him! I see him!"
And –
So, everyone comes running.
And they chase him into this mine.

And –
So the national guard now,
And all this –
All –
Have chased Rambo into this –
Abandoned mine.
And uh –
(Like a – like a coal mine.)
And like, 'cause –
So it's basically there's like a –

In the side of a mountain
There's like a little opening
Like a little sort of wooden – opening,
Where the – at the head of this –
At the head of this mine
Which leads down into the
Into the mountain.
There's the –
Like this old deserted mine.

And so Rambo's taking shelter there
'Cause all the national guard is –
There's like 50 national guard outside now
All shooting machine guns at him
And uh –
Rambo's – you know –
Shooting back at them
With his rifle, but he realizes he's really –
He's really pinned here.
And um –
Then they – they fire a uh –
They fire like –
A rocket grenade or something.
Into the opening of the mine.
And seal it off, and Ram –
Rambo kinda jumps back just in time and –
And uh –
And so now there's like
Now there's like a –
A big PILE of rubble,
Essentially,
Between Rambo,
And everyone else –
And every –
And the national guards.

But Rambo –
Rambo's still – still alive.
And he –

And so they –
He calls –
He's about to give up.
He's like "Well I – this is – this is it.
It looks like –
I guess I'm stuck.
'Cause I'm –
Caught in this mine, uh –
The – you know –
There are –
There's 50 national guard outside,
I'm caught in this mine, and
I guess the gig is up."
So –
He is about to surrender his weapon.
He – he talks to them, he says:
"Okay, alright – I'll give up."
And he's about to surrender his weapon.
And so he's pushing
Over the pile of rubble
(There's just like this little crawlspace now,
Between him and the national guard)
So, he's pushing over the pile of rubble
With his rifle, to give them up his rifle,
And then he realizes
As he does this he feels the wind,
He feels the breeze come in from the –
Front of the mine and –
And with his – with his –
Adept Green Beret skills,
He realizes that
The way the air is circling
There must be another way out the back!
Because otherwise the air wouldn't be
Drawn in this way.
So just before he gives his rifle,
He pulls it back!
And starts heading back
Down INTO the mine!

Because – because he says to himself:
"There must be another way out!"

And he is just the kinda guy
Who just does NOT give up,
You know.

And so –
He's goin' through the mine,
And he's goin' and goin', goin'
It's gettin' darker and deeper
And he – and he
And uh –
(There's another funny
Funny line, too, that I –
That I remember 'cause he says to him–
Like he's got – he's got matches
And so he makes
Like a little torch,
But he can't see very well, and um –
He – he says to himself:
"God, like I wish I had a flashlight."
And then he's –
Like he jokes to himself:
"Ah, well, for that matter
I wish I also had a –
You know a – a this and that,
And a coat, and uh – I should just
Go down to my local hardware store
And pick these things up."
Like – like a little joke in the –
In the book.
So.)

Um.

And uh –
So it – they – it's gettin'
Harder and harder to navigate

Through the cave.
He doesn't know if he's
Goin' right.
He – he figures he might just be –
Part of him is just like –
Gonna like die down there,
And just get lost.
And
He then finally –
He comes to like this little opening.
And it STINKS!
It smells really really bad!
And he realizes
He's only got one way to go,
And he's gotta go through this little opening.
And that's the only way to go
To get out
But it REALLY REALLY STINKS!
And he reaches his hand in,
And he comes back,
And it's like COVERED in SHIT!
And – it's like –
"Oh my God!"
And it's – uh –
'Cause it's BATS!
There are like Bats!
There's like this –
There are these, uh –
These sort of like –
This – this whole – like
Cluster of – you know like
A million bats
LIVE down here in this –
In this mine.

And so –
He pushes – uh.
And he realizes:
"Oh my God, I gotta crawl through

This little tunnel full of bat shit!"
And he's like –
"This is like the worst thing ever.
You know, I've been like through all this
Stuff in the war,
And I've done all this – all –
But this is – this is really fuckin' awful.
That I gotta crawl through this."
And so like – he's gotta like
Squirm his way like
Through this little
Tiny narrow passage
Like THROUGH –
This just NOXIOUS – uh –
Bat shit!

And then –!
So he gets out
And he gets into a
Kinda like the cavern.
He's covered in bat shit.
And then all the bats they –
Go BERZERK!
There's like a billion of them –
They go berserk!
And he thinks they're attacking him,
'Cause they're all flying by him,
And he's standing there,
Like up to his knees in bat shit.
And all the bats are coming at him
And he's like freaking out,
And he's just totally –
Screaming like – he's –
He's losing it.
He's just – you know – he's –
Like losing –
This is just enough for him.

But then he realizes
The bats are just flying out of the cave.
They're not attacking him.
And so he keeps – he –
So –
And he follows them.
He realizes:
"Well, okay if the bats –
If the bats are leaving
Then they must –
They've got a way out."
So he follows the bats,
And they show him the way out.
(Of course he's covered in bat shit, but,
But now he's – but now he's – uh.
He's found the way out.)

And uh –
So meanwhile –
They don't –
The rest of the peop—
The rest of like the national guard and everyone
They're wondering:
"What happened, did he –
Go into the mine?
Is he dead?
How come he didn't give up.
We thought he was giving up,
But now he didn't give up…"
Blahblahblah…
Uh –
And uh –
You know they thought that – they –
Lost him.
And they –
They figure:
"Well he's probably down in the mine
And he's dead"
And they don't know what to do,

And um –
"He's got it." – and –
So Rambo, meanwhile then is –
You know, comes out like the other
Side of the mountain or something
And slips past – slips past the – the –
The Guards there – whatever –
The people searching for him over there.
And he gets –
He gets uh – he
He steals a – uh –
A car!
And he starts to drive out of town.

And this is where the book gets really –
W–Weird.
And I haven't done a good job of –
Of talking about the psychology of the book,
But through – through this whole process
Of all this hunting –
Of back and forth –
Of Teasle and Rambo,
There's this – kinda this weird
Sorta psychological bond
Starts to happen.

This BOND.
Between Teasle and Rambo.
And Teasle really starts to really THINK like –
He tries to THINK like The Kid, and he –
And he has –
So – so – and he – he's
He's having these –
'Cause you know he's –
He's sitting on his, eh –
Teasle is – is – is –
Having these heart problems now,
And he's
He's got like a fever,

'Cause he's all fucked up from his –
From his – you know, or—
Ordeal with Rambo.
So he's like sitting on his couch,
In his office, and he's trying to all –
Look at maps
And trying to figure out
Where Rambo's going,
And what are they going to do?
And did he get away?
And what's going on now?
And he's calling his – his – wife.
His wife is calling from California,
And uh –
That whole relationship is ju–
Is shitty, and –

Uh –
And so – and then he has this –
He takes this nap.
And he –
He has this vision!
Teasle has this – and he says –
And he realizes where Rambo is!
Because like –
Somehow the psychological bond
Or something –
He just sees cars.
He sees cars, and he sees –
CARS!
And so he knows – like Ra-ra–
Teasle wakes up from his nap and says:
"I know he's still alive.
I know where he is.
I – I know where he is."
And –
Everyone's like:
"What? How can you know?
How do you know where he is?"

And he's just like – he's just like:
"I KNOW. I know now.
I know where he is."

And so –
Even though all the rest of the
Army and all the –
Volunteers and everyone –
Who are still trying to find him –
Are still out in the woods looking for him –
Teasle alone gets in his car,
And drives out to where he KNOWS
Rambo is trying to escape –
In a car!

Rambo meanwhile is
Cr—cruisin' down the road,
Thinkin' "Ah! I've finally –
You know – ah – I've gotten – uh –
You know –
Gotta – got away!
I've just gotta get – uh –
Get outta town here.
I'll ditch this car, and get another car, and –
In a couple a days I'll be in Mexico..."
(Oh and this is 'noth–
Another line I remember
From the book that I always liked very much, too, that –
'Cause they're – what –
Rambo's plan was to – to –
To go to Mexico, and he says um:
"I'm gonna go to Mexico, and –
and I'm – I'm gonna --
And every day I'm going to swim in the sea."
I'm going to swim in the sea.
Yeah.)

And uh –

So THEN – !
And then outta nowhere!

So he's headed –
He's headed out the main road of town.
Like no – no one around.
'Cause all – all the police and
Everyone else is back in the woods,
Where they THINK he is…
And there –
In the middle of no –
Standing in the middle of the street
Is just Teasle.
With his gun.
His Browning.
Nine Millimeter.
And uh –
(That carries thirteen bullets.)
And
He starts shooting
At Rambo.
Through the windshield.
Of the car.

And –
I think he hits him?
No, he doesn't hit him, but he –
But he – Rambo's gotta
S-slam on the brakes,
And he wacks his head
Against the uh –
No, he does!
Yeah!
He shoots him once!
He gets hit once.
And –
He – and his head kinda
Goes through the windshield,
Or hits the radio.

'Cause he's got this huge gash
Across his forehead.
And.
Uh.
And he crashes.
And he's like: "Holy shit!"
You know,
"It's Teasle.
Again."

And so he climbs out of the car,
And Teasle, you know,
Comes right after him!
Is shooting at him.
And Rambo shh – Rambo shoots at him!
So now they're in the middle of the –
Like a – residential neighborhood
Shooting at each other!

And Ra – you know – Rambo's all
Fucked up, he's got these –
Broken ribs,
He's been shot once,
His head bashed open,
He is covered in bat shit,
You know…

And Teasle is not too great either,
Because he's – you know –
He's on the verge of having a heart attack,

So they're shootin' at each other.
In like – ah – you know –
Out in someone's like – lawn.

And uh.

Rambo hits Teasle.
Shoots him.

Up through the stomach.
And Teasle falls back.
He's not dead but he's –
He's been hit, and he's –
So he's lying on the ground.

And so Rambo – I mean, but uh –
Rambo is really fucked up,
And he's losing a lot of blood.
And – but he's STILL – !
He's still going!
He's like –
He CRAWLS out from the like the –
You know –
From this residential neighborhood,
He crawls into this field.
And –
It's THORNS!
It's the –
Just like the same thorns that –
That Teasle escaped from!
And the end of this chapter,
I remember very specifically,
Ends with Rambo thinking:
"Well, if –"
Rambo thinks to himself:
"Well, if Teasle could escape
Through thorns why couldn't he?"

And so –
Rambo starts just dragging himself.
Like he – you know –
He's –
Been shot now,
And he's just a –
But he's like dragging himself with his arms
Through – through these thorns.
Still thinking that he can –
Get away.

And meanwhile now,
The rest of the police,
Everyone realizes that –
What's going on downtown here.
So the rest of the police
And Trautman and every –
And everyone come back
To where Teasle is.
And they find Teasle
Lying on the sidewalk there shot
And –
(No! He's still alive!)
And they –
And they're like –
"Don't – you know – don't move or –
We're gonna –
We've got a stretcher coming.
Don't move!"
And he says like:
"No! Oh! It's gotta be me!
Don't kill him!
It's gotta be me!
I – I—I've gotta be the one to kill him.
Don't – "
And uh –
Because they start –
The policemen start chasing –
What they see
This trail of blood,
They see Rambo's off crawling
Through the –
Through the thorn bushes
Tryin' to get away still.
And uh –
But – and Teasle's like:
"No! No!
Don't kill him!
It's gotta be me!
It's gotta be me!"

And it's like he drags him –
He drags himself up
Even though he's been shot.
(He's like on the verge of death,
I mean…)
He drags himself up, and
He starts to stumble, and
They're all sayin' to him like:
"No! Stay!
We've got a stretcher for you!
If you're shot, you know,
You need to stay –"
But he starts to drag himself through the –
Through the thorns, too,
'Cause he wants to –
He wants it to be HIM to get –
To get Rambo.

But at this point, too,
It's like this weird…

Yeah!
Well they're tellin' him to – to – to –
Stay – to stay down,
But he's like pushing them off,
And he's like – and he's –
Kinda struggles to his feet, and like
Trautman's telling him to
"Stay down! You've been shot."
But he's like –
"No, no, it's gotta be me."
And he's – gotta go and,
He wants it to be – to be –
Like – the – this – this –
This is the weird sort of torning –
TURNING point, too, in that –
Where there's –
A weird sort of relationship
Between Teasle and Rambo

Is starting to come out where
It's gone –
It has TRANSCENDED
Just the revenge.
That it's like they –
These two men have been LOCKED
In this sort of –
This – this sort of battle that –
That – that has now gone so far,
And it's been so painful that it –
It goes –
It – it becomes like –
Biblical proportions or something.
It's just – it has TRANSCENDED
Just the simple r – r – Revenge.
There's this sorta RESPECT,
This – this sort of FAMILIAL HONOR
Or something that's GROWN
Outa this – St – s –
The – this – eh –
Monumental Struggle.

And so.
Uh.
He just –
Finally –
So he's tryin' to –
You know –
Rambo's dragging himself through the –
Through the thorns,
And um.

And Teasle's tryin' to struggle after him.
And – and Trautman
Trautman just – uh –
Sees Rambo,
And uh.
Uh.
And – and – and then –

And uh –
Uh –
Teasle collapses.
He just can't move anymore.
And he hears this loud
BANG!

And Trautman comes back.
And he says, you know:
"What's going on? Where is he?"
And he says:
"Well, I just – I just –
Took the top of his head off
With a shotgun."
I JUST TOOK THE TOP OF HIS HEAD OFF
WITH A SHOTGUN.
Traut – Trautman killed –
Kills Rambo.

Uh.
But he – and he –
And he comes back to Teasle
Who is laying there
Bleeding to death,
To tell him:
Like –
"I just – I – I – I killed him."
And – and he –
Teasle asks him how –
"How was it for you?"
And Trautman says:
"Better. Better than –
When I knew he was in pain."

And so Trautman's just lying there,
(I mean TEASLE's just lying there)
He –
He knows that he's –
You know –

Bleeding to death.
And he just has this great sort of
Transcendental Moment where
He just –
Uh –
He just FEELS – uh –
Like a complete sense of –
Of –
PEACE.
And –
And – and
(This is the line I remember
Best
From the book is –)
So then Trautman pumped
The empty shotgun shell,
Out of the gun that he just used to –
To shoot –
To blow off Rambo's head.
And it says –
The line is something like:
"And as – as – as the shell,
Uh, like –
Gently arc'ed through the air,
Uh.
Teasle –
Like lay – lay there –
And FLOODED WITH LOVE
For The Kid,
And died."
And that's the last
Line of the book.

Phffffhhhh.

Uh.

Well, to me it's ahh –
I don't –
You know I mean it's just
It's very – very beautiful.
It's one of –
To me, it's literally –
It's like one of the most
Beautiful moments in all of literature.

I mean, 'cause –
Because it's – uh.
The fact that this –
That this –
You know it's all this –
It's – you know, it's a –
It's kind of a PULP book.
Yeah.
It's not – you know –
Obviously it's not what
Many people would consider
Grand Literature,
But it –
But for ME, it –
It is just as Grand, and just as –
Universal as – as – as Hamlet
Or anything like that, because
It's –
This –
BOND
That forms between them,
This sort of
Bizarre –
Father Son bond
That happens
When you're trying to kill each other
TRYING TO KILL EACH OTHER
While they were trying to kill each other

Yeah! Yeah!

In other words – in other words,
The struggle was so monumental,
And Teasle's life became so wrapped up in it
In such a short amount of time,
In other words it became his –
This was his salvation.
In a way.
To – to me it's like –
'Cause his life –
He's like this middle-aged guy,
His life was kinda shitty,
He's just –
Like the sheriff of this small town,
His marriage is falling apart.
He was a bored, kinda lonely guy.
Uh.
And –
This –
In – in a – in a way,
The – the way I take it, then is –
Is Teasle –
This was kinda a salvation –
It was a redemptive thing
For him.

And he dies at the end,
As most people do, and –
Uh.
But he –
But he does not
Die –
He does not die –
Uh –
EMPTY.
You know – he – he
His life is –
Has been
FULFILLED.
And he

Had this
Son,
In a way.
And he uh –
Um.
He –
This –
Struggle that he had been through,
Brought him to, you know –
This mortal enemy,
That he's been trying to kill,
He uh somehow –
Something SLIPS!
Something CHANGES in his mind,
Something –
Because they were both drawn into this –
Struggle of Biblical Proportions! –
He came to
LOVE him.
Because he somehow saved his –
I don't – I don't know!
Like he um –
Ah –
I don't know!
It gave him,
In the end some
Greater sense of purpose.
Or something.
And um.
Uh.

That's just an extremely
Poignant
Poignant –
Moment.
Uh.
It's like – um.
It's like –
There's – there's something about the all –

What really gets me about someone who –
Who KNOWS they're going to die,
And they're about to die,
But
They have this great sense of relief,
And this sense of contentment,
And they are flooding with love.
Because it's –
Now it's okay that they are going to die.
They – they –
They – they did not
They – it – it –
And – or their life wasn't in – in –
In vain.
They – they –
Uh.
They reached some kind of answer.
Some kind of conclusion.
E – even if the answer,
Or the conclusion
Was that there is no answer or conclusion,
But they
Then
Reached it.
And –
There's the sense of great relief,
There's the sense of how –
How Beautiful
Everything is,
And this real –
Just this real sense of –
The Pervasive –
LOVE! –
That seems to happen
Right before the –
The moment of death.

That's my

Uh.

Interpretation.
Uh.
But that's what –
What always, uh –
What always gets me,
You know.

Yep.

So Yeah.

I think you should read it.
Yeah.

(And you should watch the movie, too,
It's not as –
You know, it's not as good,
But there's – uh.
Something to be said for it.)

Yeah – that's, you know –
Kinda the –
The unfortunate thing,
You might say,
About having –
You know, seeing uh –
A film version of a book, is it –
Inevitably,
As you're reading it,
(Or then describing it as I just did)
Inevitably
Those
Visuals come back to you.

But at the same time, too,
Though, I created a lot of –
Because the book is very different,
It describes Rambo as very different,
It describes this –
The descriptions are very different.
You get –
I have very vivid
Pictures in my mind,
Just from the book.

So now, as I describe it,
I get sort of a –
A uh –
COLLAGE
Of – of – of – of Stallone images
From the movie,
And my own personal images
From the book.

You know, it – it get –
Because eh – it's –
It's a book that – that –
Yeah, yeah –
It's a lot of –
It's a lot of macho action stuff,
But there's – there's a real
It's not just like a
PULP
ACTION
MACHO
Sort of thing –
This – this guy –
This author
David Morrell,
Actually had some –
Some talent in terms of
Getting at –
Some real human

Uh.
Some real human insights,
I – I think.
And –

And so –

The –
Eh,
Well, like, as I said,
The – the book is almost you know in a way
Flushes out the character of Teasle
Even more so than Rambo,
Rambo – er – Teasle
Is more of a three dimensional character than –
Than Rambo is, in the book.
It's actually more about Teasle,
And his – his struggle,
You know, to try and capture the kid,
And the sort of redemptive
Thing that happens to him
At the end.

Uh,
So that's – that's missing, and
Again, in the movie
He's just – he's played
Rather poorly by
Uh
Brian Dennehy.
(Well, though, Brian Dennehy,
He's o – he's okay, I guess,
I don't know.
I don't know how to judge acting anymore,
So.)

Uh.
But um.
Ah –

He's just a very flat character.
In the – in the uh –
You know –
All that's just kinda glossed over,
Of course, in the –
In the movie,
And it just –
You know, the movie is
You know, the big Stallone blockbuster
That was more about
EXPLOSIONS
And MUSCLES
Than – than an – any kind of
Psychological drama.

Uh, but the book goes into a lot of detail
About –
About Rambo's time in Vietnam,
And Teasle's time in the Korean War,
And uh.
Yeah.
And their struggles –
There
And how it
Affected both of them, and –
Um.
Uh.

Uh.
Yeah!
Yeah!
I think, you know –
I'm sure –
That there – there are a few other details,
Specific details, that –
That are coming back to me now, as I –
I think, but I gave you a pretty good overall –
I mean, 'cause I've read it –
Read it a lot, and – and I –

And – and it's a book whose details I have
Always been very fascinated
With
And so like I memorized
(not INTENTIONALLY,
But I know that I –)
Like I memorized –
Like the WEAPONS that they use,
Like I refer to his –
Teasle's GUN
Is this Nine Millimeter
Browning gun that holds thirteen bullets,
And I was always very fascinated
As a kid
By how many bullets a gun can hold.
And I always thought that was quite –
Quite something
That this gun –
Gun held thirteen bullets,
And Rambo KNEW it held thirteen bullets.

Um.

Sure, I woulda – but –
I never had a – a gun.
I had a small 22 rifle,
But I think my Dad took it
Somewhere, um.
But – but no, I've never had –
I would LIKE to have –
Have a gun.
I'm very fascinated by –
By guns and weaponry, and that's –
A – a lot of the book go –
GOES into great detail
Describing
The Weapons.
And um.
That was always a

Big plus.
For me.

ONE
MAJOR
DIFFERENCE
Between the book
And the film:
The film introduced this –
This – this KNIFE!
That Rambo had,
That was just like this
Revolutionary
Badass
Green Beret Knife!
That was like really BIG
And serrated on one edge,
And they – the –
The hol – handle of it was HOLLOW!
And he kept matches in it,
And a – a needle and thread,
And like in the movie he –
Instead of breaking his ribs
When he falls off the cliff,
He cuts his arm really badly,
And so it – in the –
In the film they show him
Taking a needle and thread
Out of his Knife
And sewing up his arm.

Um.

And uh.

And all through the BOOK!
As I was reading the Book,
I kept waitin' for them to
Talk about this KNIFE!

It's like:
"Why-don't-they-talk-about-the-knife?
Why-don't-they-talk-about-the-knife?"
And they never talk about the knife!
And I realized then
That that knife was
Was created for the –
For the movie.
And um.

But uh.
So that's –
That's one detail that I
Actually liked from the –
From the movie
That was not in the book,
This – this really,
'Cause I – I like knives,
You know I collect –
Collect knives and –
And I, then,
As a teenager
Collected a – a lot of these
Fake Rambo knives,
And I always got these knives that were
Serrated on one edge and had
Um – a hollow –
Hollow handle
Where I could keep
Matches and um –
Fishing line
And needles and I put –
I put inside mine
I have all the things that uh –
All the things that Rambo had in –
Had inside his knife.

Oh yeah!
Uh, yeah.

I've got –
Yeah, I've got a few.
I've even got one of them here
In New York, with me.
I've got a few.

Ha ha ha!

No, 'cause I might have to wage
A one man war some –
Someday out in Central Park,
Yeah.
And when I do,
I'm gonna have that knife with me,
So I can –
So I can sew my uh –
Heh!
Sew myself up!

Yeah.
Well it could, yeah.
It could happen.

Ha ha!

Yeah.

Yeah.

Yeah.

Yeah it takes a –
Takes a lot out of me.
Yeah.

Uh –
I would love to at some point
Do – like the –
A film.

It's always been my dream
To make like a honest –
Like a –
Like a true –
True to the novel sort of adaptation
Of First Blood without all the –
You know – Hollywood.

In – in fact did you know they – they
Ram –
They – they kept Rambo –
In – in the original film,
When they filmed it – Rambo
Rambo did die in the end of the film, too.
And they test marketed it on
Audiences,
And audiences didn't like it,
'Cause it's just – you know –
A sad ending because
Rambo died at the end.
(And also I guess they realized
They couldn't have a sequel.)
So they changed it!
They went back,
And re-filmed the ending
Where Rambo doesn't die in the film.
And so, of course, and
They can make Rambo –
You know.
And – and – !
You know that – there's –
And so they made 2 and 3.
2 was a really big hit.
3, not so much.
And now, you know now
That Stallone's back in shape,
And he just made –
And he just made Rocky 6,
He's uh –

He's back at –
He's makin' Rocky –
Rambo 4!
You know?

So after the first movie
He's – the –
The only characters that – that –
That went on in the film,
After the first book, were just Rambo
And Trautman.
(And – although, uh –
Richard Crenna
Who plays – uh – Trautman,
Died a few years ago.
So he won't be in the new –
The new Rambo film.)

But there are the real –
You know – I'll go.
I'll go and – I'll go and see it,
Because uh –
You know, I'm just –
This is –
I've got such an attachment to this.
From my childhood.
But I go – gotta admit,
You know, Stallone is just –
Like –
Just makes a complete –
Complete circus out of –
Out of, uh –
True Art.

And uh –
So it's always been my –
MY DREAM, to uh –
To remake that novel
In its – in its – original

Sort of
GRITTY
Psychological, um –
Uh.
Duh – um.
Or – original FORM.

Although, I think I'm getting –
You know –
And I always thought, too, like –
Well, that I'd play –
I'd play Rambo.
But now I – now I think I'm
Getting too old, so –
And it's probably gonna take me –
Prob'ly be 20 or 30 years anyway
Before I'm able to do it,
So –
I'll prob'ly have to –
I'll like –
Prob'ly play Teasle.

I don't know.
I'll get, you know –
I'll get some 22 year old –
Kid.

That's what I'll have to –
Yeah.
I'll –
Prob'ly have to play Teasle.
I'll prob'ly play Teasle.
Ya, I'll probably –
'Cause I probably won't be able to
Make it until I'm middle-aged
Anyways.

But then –
But I shouldn't then – what –

No, I – no!
If I – if I want to honestly want to be
TRUE to the whole thing,
Then I shouldn't be –
'Cause – you know,
Neither Rambo NOR Teasle
Should be really –
Super buff.
You know.

That's all Hollywood –
Bullshit.

I might –
I might stop working out, if I –
Yeah!
If I can make my First Blood film –
I might, uh –
I might stop workin' out,
So I can –
Yeah. Yeah.

Yeah.

Like the characters,
Like if you're playing such a –
Such a character, then you gotta –
Kinda look like them, er –
You – you know,
Like – like when they make a
Movie about
Richard Nixon or something,
Like they try and make the actor –
Like an – actor that kinda looks like
Richard Nixon, that's –
Yeah. Yeah.

Yeah.

So, but – but there's –
Like there's –
This – this First Blood project –
This –
I – is like the one –
The one place though where I
Feel like that sort of traditionalism,
I still hold to –
To heart.
Where –
Whereas like any other kind of project
Or acting thing that I would do,
I would – you know, ALL –
It would be much more of a – a –
Relevatory approach,
But – but it –
But this – thing about this is
It's like it calls for – it –
It uh.
It calls for um.
Uh –
INTENSE – uh.
Realism.
Of that sort.

He gives a good des –
Pretty good physical description of
Rambo, I mean and –
In the book he's just –
He's this –
Kinda SKINNY kid!
You know he's not all muscular, or –
You know, I – I think of him as
Prob'ly like a real ectomorph.
Prob'ly built kinda like –

And he's got uh –
So he's really –
You know, real – really

Strong!
But not like
BIG muscles.
Just –
Really LEAN, and –
And strong.
And uh.
Of course, all these –
Criss-crossed scars all over his chest
From being uh –
From being tortured.

And um –
Oh! It also says in the book,
I remember this –
He has like a black
A triangular patch of black hair
On his chest.
That's a –
And um –
Uh –
And I uh see him with black –
(I wish that I could really –
That I was sure of that.
I think it was black hair –
Yeah, black –)
And the thing is, too,
I always pictured him then as
Running through the woods with –
'Cause like they KINDA
Start to cut his hair, and
Kinda start to trim his –
You know, cut his –
Cut his beard, but –
Before he goes berserk!
So he must have like this really –
Fucked up
Hair cut.
Where like half of it's kinda shaved,

But some of it's there,
And it's a – long beard, but –
Some of it's gone, and –
So.
Um.

And uh –
And I see him, too –
Like I don't really have a specific picture
Of – of his – face.
I never really –
Have that when I read a novel.
I never really –
See the character's face?
But –
But I know that it's a very sort of um –

It's not like mine.
It's a very –

A – average –
He doesn't have a big nose.
He doesn't have a big nose like me.
He's got –
It's a very sort of
AVERAGE AMERICAN face.

Like –
You know, like this – um –
You know
Any G – guy, right?
Young guy you'd run into
In the Midwest and stuff.
It's just that kind of –
Uh –

Uh –

You know,
Not – not European looking.

Small nose –
Ehuh.
Kinda square jawed, small nosed.
Um.

That just sort of –
TYPICAL!
Handsome –
Stereotypical
General
HANDSOME
Kind of –
Kind of – look.
I guess.

If I were playing Rambo, phff –
Uh –

I – I think I couldn't –
Um.
I mean that would –
It's one thing to sort of –
You know,
Al – alter your –
Your body one way,
But I don't think that I could, um –
(Without like SERIOUS –
Like makeup – and –
So that I'd need like a huge budget…)
But I don't –
I don't think that is –
As important.
That wouldn't be as important to me.
I could –
I could play Rambo,
Looking like I do now,

And it would be fine.

Yeah.

If I play Teasle?
Well that'll be –
I'm probably built more like
Te – Teasle any –
You know Teasle I think of as more of –
Probably like a shorter
Kinda stocky guy
Any – anyway.
Um.
And so I'm probably naturally
More built like – like –
Although he – he, too
Would be –
Have a more –
More of a sorta typical
American Midwestern look
He wouldn't look –
Really look kinda Jewish
Like – like me, but.
But um.
But – but again.
That's –
That's something that
I won't be as –
So –
Concerned with.

I thought about –
I thought about actually
Making this movie –
This film –
In my apartment.
Just by myself!
And like –
Just saying like:

"Okay!" like –
(You know,
As – as we do with our limitations...)
Just say like:
"Alright, I don't have –
A mountain.
I don't have a forest.
I don't have actors.
I don't have –
ANYTHING.
I just have my little –
Apartment in Manhattan.
And my camera.
Can I make –
First Blood?
Can I make the film I want to make?
Here in my apartment?"

And I would play all the parts!
And I – I would just use
Different parts of my apartment,
To represent the different –
Mountains,
The town...
You know what I mean?

Hello?

D'ya know what I mean?
So, yeah, I could do it if –
Yeah, as a one-man film.

I mean I could just
Set my camera up on a tripod
And – and stuff –
And just –
R – run around in my apartment
And like play all the –
Play all the roles,

You know, and –
And make –
You know I could make –
Like my loft bed, I could make that
Into the cliff that he's gotta
Climb down and –
And jump off of
And um.

You know –
There's a lot of possibilities.

Yeah.

And um.

Yeah, no –
I think I could –
I've been – yeah.
I've been thinking about that for a while.
That'd be a good project for me to do.
I think.
Or – you know,
And I could work on it –
Whenever, you know –
Work on it late at night
(If I wasn't too loud) and –
Um.
I could dub in – I could dub in –
I could dub in sound later,
Yeah.

Yeah.
No, I think it'd be – uh.
I think it'll be –
Good, I mean I'll –
It could be like –

Yeah!

No, I wouldn't just toss it –
Toss it together!

Uh.
I mean it –
Takes a lot of –
Preparation, and uh –
And, I mean, of course
I'd approach it with uh – with –
I mean it'd be my greatest role –
To date!
I'd be – It'd be –
Just an acting tour de force!
I would – I would just, uh –
I'd play all these characters, and –
Uh.
To the –
You know, to the –
Fullest Extent, and –

I mean it's a very masculine –
Very masculine –
NOVEL.
It –
Just about every way you look at it.
There's very little –
Uh.
The only woman in it, really, is –
Is ANNA.
Willfred Teasle's –
Wife.
Who he – who he calls occasionally,
Who he's – who he's ESTRANGED from.
There's very little feminine perspective
In the book.
I would say.

I think my whole life's work
Probably IS gonna be somehow

Tied –
Tied to this.
But.
But I think that there's –
At least the film, the version
I make in my apartment
Might be –
(Well!? I don't know –
Maybe that'll be the whole – yeah!
Or it might just be a sort of a –
The – the – the forerunner…)
Of the – of the MAJOR work.
Uh.

Which is when I actually do
The whole –
You know, like ON LOCATION in –
In Kentucky.
When I actually shoot it,
You know.

(ahem)

With a budget of – you know.
Sixty Million Dollars.
Yeah.

Plus – I like a one-man film.
I might prefer that anyway,
Because I can't – you know
I hate workin' with actors.
So.

Ha ha ha!

Yeah.

end

Stills from the video of Rambo Solo

Video by Peter Nigrini, featuring Zachary Oberzan

In the live performance, three simultaneous videos of Oberzan performing the monologue in his apartment are projected behind the actor who synchs both his movement and vocals to the projected video tracks.

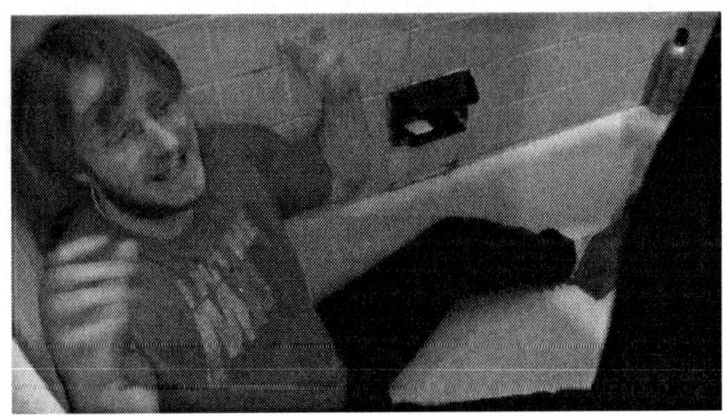

53rd State Press publishes new plays, performance texts, and experimental documentary dance pamphlets.

For information and ordering, please visit
www.53rdstatepress.com

To learn more about Nature Theater of Oklahoma, visit
www.oktheater.org

Book design and editing: Karinne Keithley
Video stills, cover and interior: Peter Nigrini

53SP 1 The Book of the Dog
53SP 2 Joyce Cho Plays
53SP 3 Nature Theater of Oklahoma's No Dice
53SP 4 Nature Theater of Oklahoma's Rambo Solo

upcoming titles:

When You Rise Up: performance texts by Miguel Gutierrez
The Mayor of Baltimore and Anthem: plays by Kristen Kosmas